SYMBOLS OF US INDEPENDENCE

THE DECLARATION OF INDEPENDENCE

US History for Kids
Children's History Books

BABY PROFESSOR

EDUCATION KIDS

In this book, we're going to talk about the American Flag and the Articles of Confederation. So, let's get right to it!

Battle of Guiliford Courthouse, 15th of March 1781

A NEW COUNTRY IS BORN

The American Revolution lasted from 1775 to 1783. The British colonies in America wanted to be free from British rule and this is why they rebelled. The governing body of the colonies decided that they needed a flag to display these new united colonies. On June 14, 1777, a resolution was passed in Congress regarding the creation of a flag. Today we still celebrate Flag Day on June 14.

This new flag was going to have thirteen stripes, seven red and six white, which alternated. There would also be a blue area that displayed thirteen white stars. The number thirteen was important because it represented the number of colonies. The description of the flag wasn't precise at that time, so several different designs were drawn up.

Surrender of Lord Cornwallis

Betsy Ross

Legend has it that Betsy Ross was responsible for sewing the first American flag. General George Washington visited her in the summer of 1777 to discuss creating a flag for the new nation. The Revolutionary War hadn't been won yet at this time.

The Continental Congress with Washington's help had come up with the basic idea, but according to the story, Betsy made some

of her own alterations on the design. She wanted the stars to have five points instead of six.

Her reasoning was that the cloth for the stars could be cut by using a single snip. The stars were arranged in a circle. No one knows if any of these details about the first flag are actually true since the details weren't made public until almost a century afterwards.

It may have taken a while for the flag's design to be finalized. There's a famous painting of George Washington completed in 1779 that shows six-pointed stars on the flag.

George Washington

None of these details about the first flag can be verified, but what is known is that Betsy Ross stitched flags for the rest of her life. Some of the flags she made were huge

18 by 24 foot sizes. At this point in time it was too early for people to have a reverence for the flag, so that is probably why there are no records providing us with the real details.

Since the first US flag was created, the design has changed at least 25 times. Some designs only lasted for one or two years but others lasted for 20 years or more. New stars were added as new groups of states were added to the Union. The last states to enter the Union were Alaska and Hawaii.

ere are some of the major changes the flag went through:

* In 1794, the design was changed to 15 stars and 15 stripes for two new states.

* In 1818, the design was changed again. This time, the stripes were changed back to represent the 13 colonies and the stars remained at 15, one for each state.

20 stars Flag

First flight of Old Glory

★ In 1912, the flag was changed so that the proportions were specified. The stars would be arranged in six rows going across with eight stars in each row. Each star was oriented with one point directly vertical.

★ In 1959, the design was changed to the one we know today with nine rows of stars across and eleven rows arranged vertically. The rows are staggered.

The 50-star version of the flag is the one we have today. There is a white star for every state. The modern design with the stars arranged in offset rows was created in 1958 by Robert G. Heft, a seventeen year old boy from Ohio. He only received a B- on his project, but his teacher changed his grade to an A after his design was chosen! This is the only one of the flag designs that has lasted 50 years.

Star-Spangled Banner

WHAT ARE THE NICKNAMES FOR THE FLAG?

The flag of the United States is the only official name of the flag but Americans have quite a few nicknames for the flag. The nicknames are:

- ★ Old Glory
- ★ The Red, White, and Blue
- ★ The American Flag
- ★ The Star-Spangled Banner
- ★ The Stars and Stripes
- ★ The United States Flag

THE NATIONAL ANTHEM

The National Anthem of the United States is a song called "The Star-Spangled Banner." It was composed by Francis Scott Key during the War of 1812. It took a while for the song to become popular and be adopted as the National Anthem. It was inspired by a huge flag that was still waving after heavy bombardment by the British.

Francis Scott Key

WHY WE HONOR THE FLAG

The flag is a symbol of independence, patriotism, and freedom. Many people have sacrificed their lives so that the citizens of America can have the freedom to live their lives in peace and harmony.

The Articles of Confederation was a precursor to the United States constitution. This simply means that it was a document designed to help the original thirteen states of the United States to govern themselves before the Constitution became law.

We the People

insure domestic Tranquility, provide for the c

and our Posterity, do ordain and establish t

All legislative Powers he

of Represe

In those days, communication over distances wasn't easy or quick. The leaders of the new nation wanted to have a document that all the colonies, now called states, could agree to. They wanted to have rules for the military, the legislature, and the common currency.

The document was written during the session of the Second Continental Congress. Each colony had a representative at the session so thirteen men were involved in its creation.

Declaration of Independence

John Dickinson

The committee chairman was John Dickinson. He was the major writer of the articles. The idea for the articles had been around since 1775. Benjamin Franklin had written a very early draft in which he entitled the union of the states as the "United Colonies of North America."

In order for the Articles of Confederation to become law, they had to be approved by all the states. The documents were sent out at the end of 1777. Virginia was the first state to approve the documents and Maryland was the last in 1781. The state of Maryland was involved in a dispute over their borders and this was why they took so long to sign.

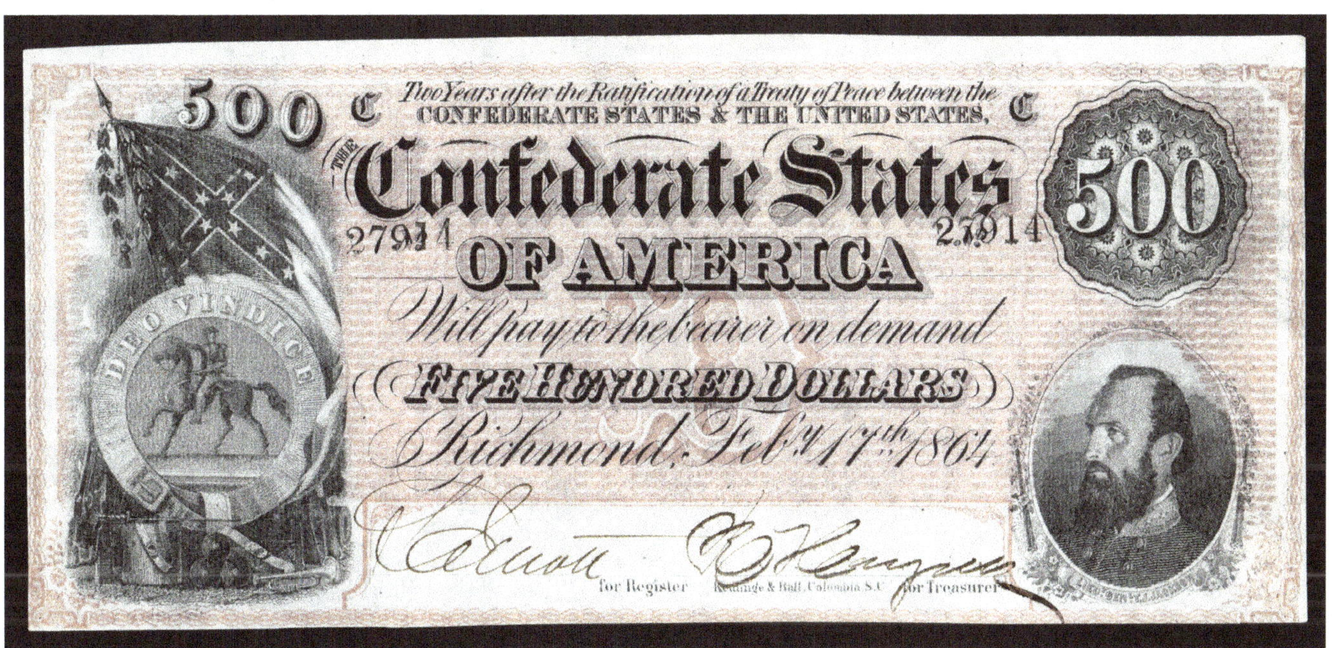

Legacy printed in bills

ARTICLES

OF

Confederation

AND

Perpetual Union

BETWEEN THE

STATES

OF

New Hampshire, Massachusetts Bay, Rhode Island, and Providence Plantations, Connecticut, New York, New Jersey, Pennsylvania, Delaware, Maryland, Virginia, North Carolina, South Carolina, and Georgia.

WILLIAMSBURG:
Printed by ALEXANDER PURDIE.

The original articles contained the thirteen articles followed by a conclusion and a section for the representatives of each colony to sign. Here is a quick summary of the intent of each article.

Article 1: The new country was named "The United States of America."

Article 2: Each state should have the power to rule itself and remain independent and free, except in cases where the rule was adopted by all states in the Confederation as a governing body.

Article 3: The states would gather together when needed to fend off enemies that could potentially take away their freedoms.

Commemorative stamp

Article 4: A citizen of the United States could move from state to state freely. If a citizen committed an offense in one state and then moved to avoid prosecution, he would be sent back to the state where the crime was committed for a trial.

Article 5: Each state holds one vote that can be cast during the session of the United States in Congress assembled. Each state can attend the Congress with up to seven delegates. Each

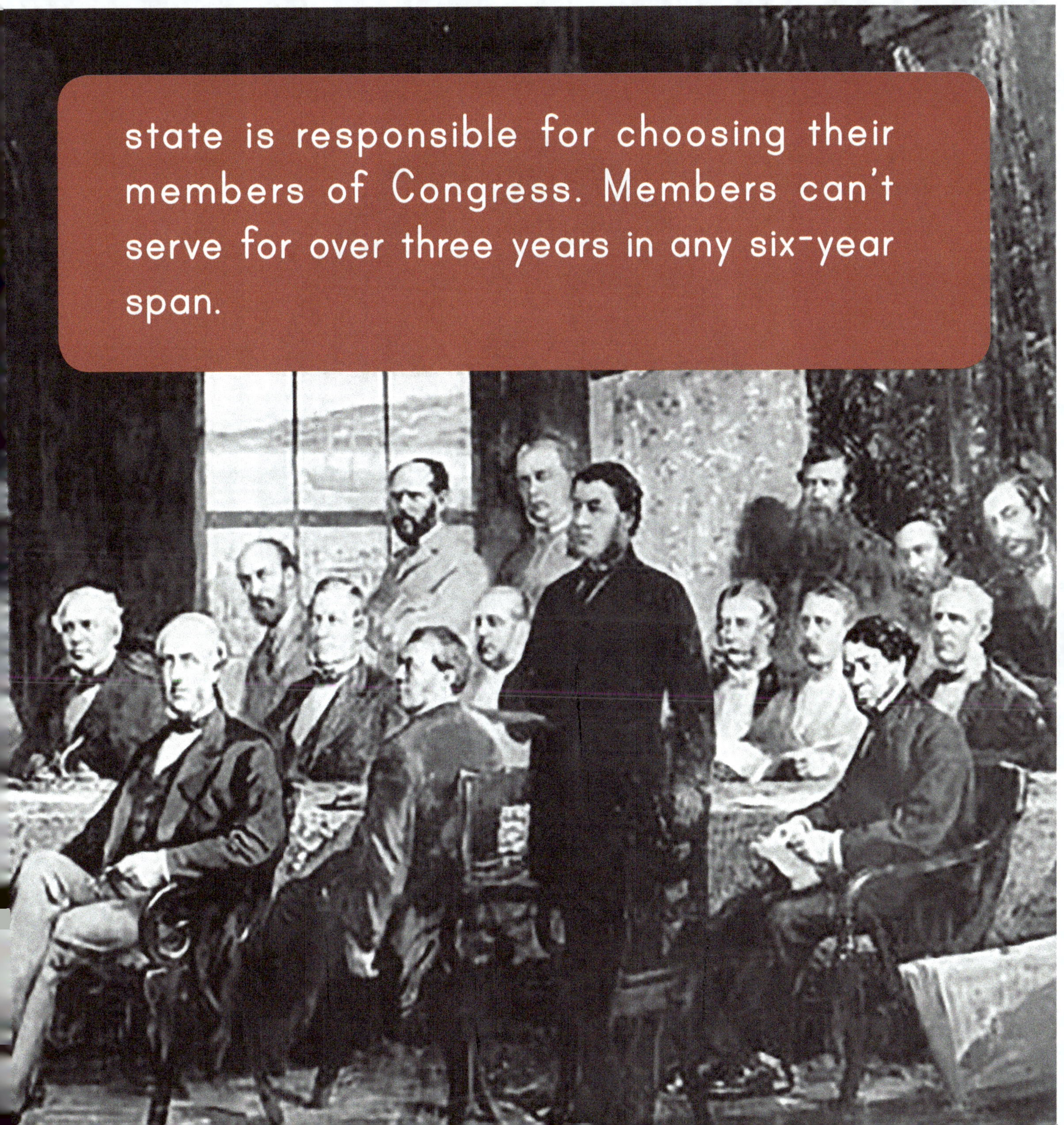
state is responsible for choosing their members of Congress. Members can't serve for over three years in any six-year span.

ALEXANDER HAMILTON
One of the Founding Fathers of the United States

Article 6: Only the government of the union of all the states can create foreign policy or declare a war. Each state can have military forces but the agreement of how to use that force must come from the central government.

Article 7: The states will be responsible for establishing the ranks within their military.

Article 8: The United States will pay for goods and services by using state-raised funds.

Article 9: The central government has only three powers: to establish war with an enemy if needed, to set the standards for currency, and to serve as a negotiating party in state-to-state disagreements.

Article 10: A committee made up of the states will govern when Congress is not in session.

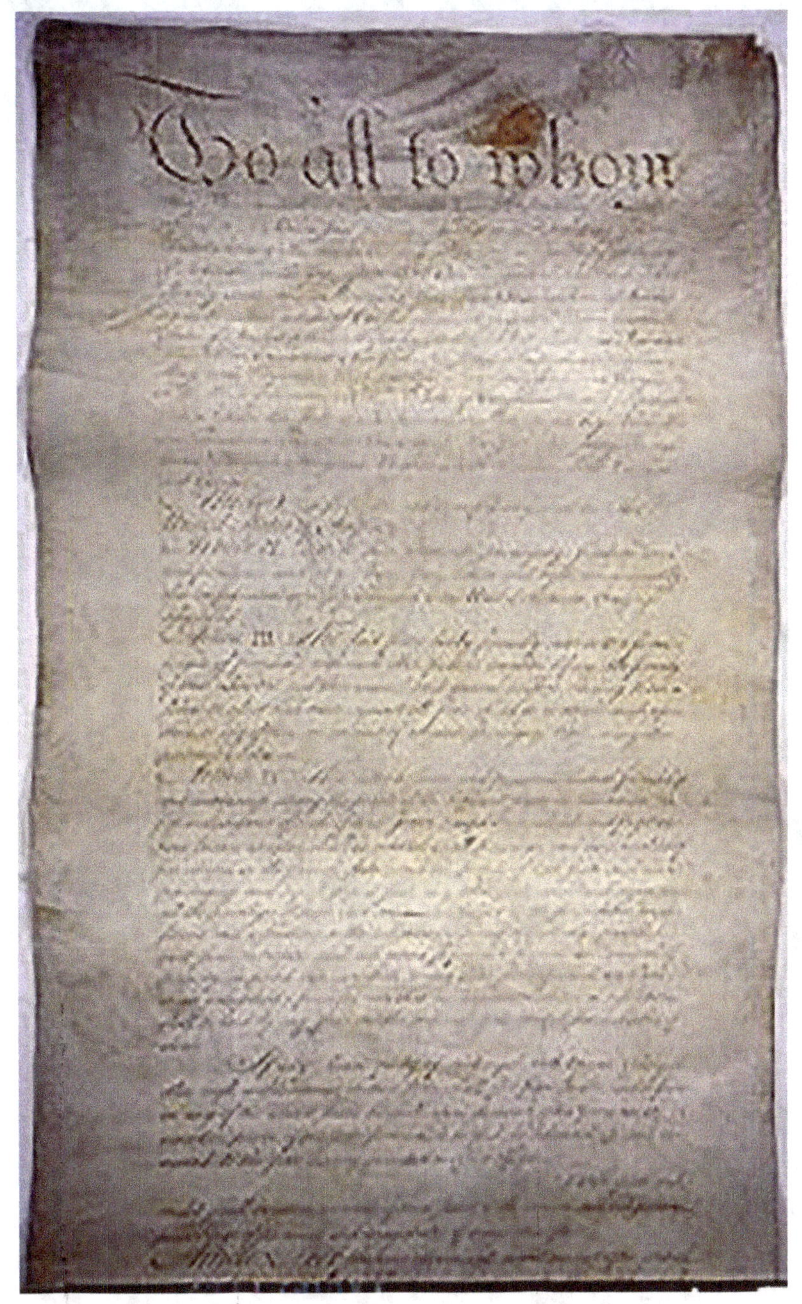

The Original articles of Confederation document

Article 11: Nine of the thirteen states must approve any new state that wishes to join.

Article 12: War debt from previous wars must be paid off.

Article 13: The articles can be amended only if all states agree.

The official title of the articles was the "Articles of Confederation and Perpetual Union." The articles sufficed as a ruling document while the country was still forming. However, after the Revolutionary War was won, the new country needed a more thorough document.

The signing of the U.S. Constitution

United States Capitol

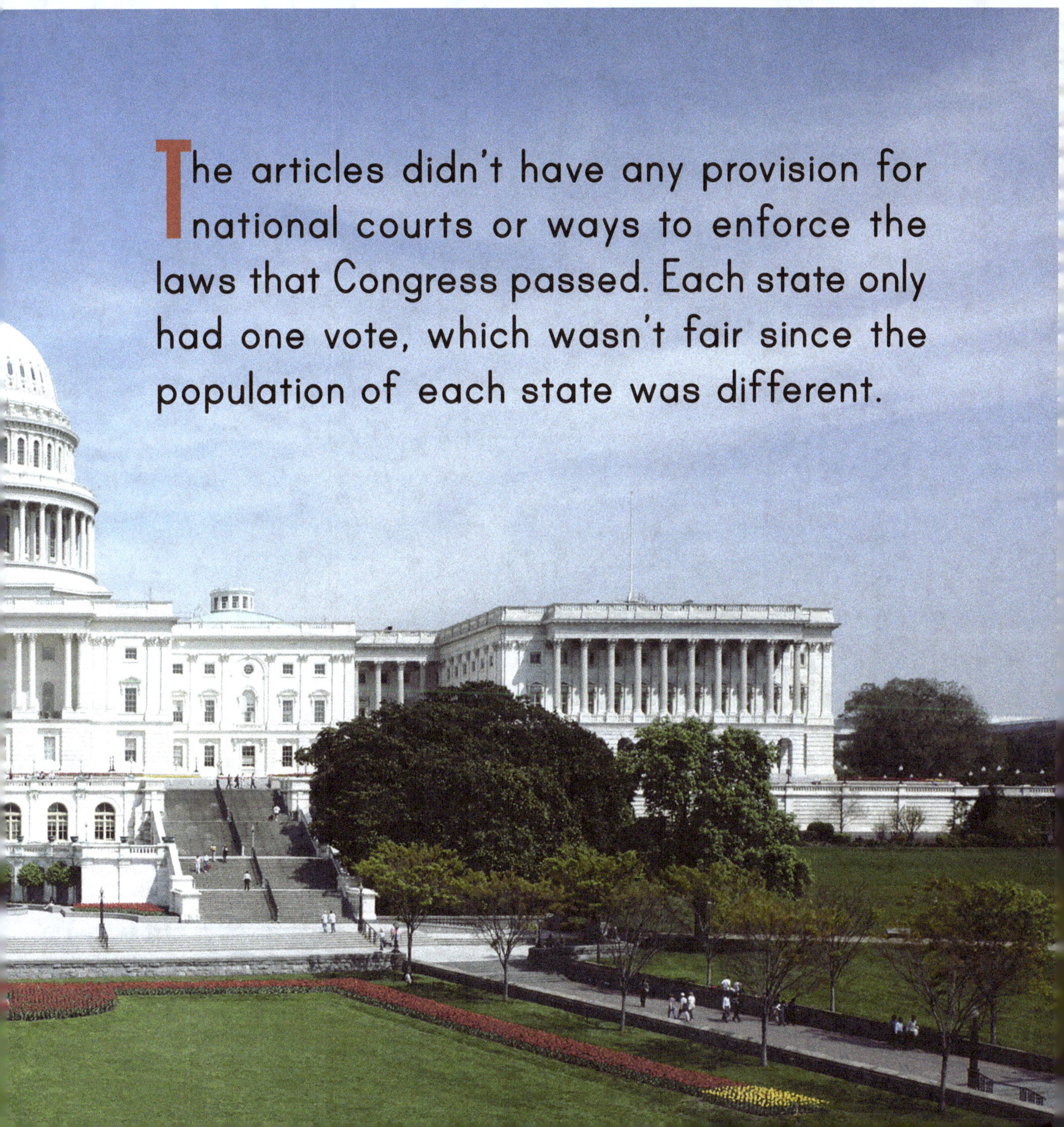
The articles didn't have any provision for national courts or ways to enforce the laws that Congress passed. Each state only had one vote, which wasn't fair since the population of each state was different.

Awesome! Now you know more about these two symbols of US independence. You can find more History Nonfiction books from Baby Professor by searching the website of your favorite book retailer.

Visit
BABY PROFESSOR
EDUCATION KIDS
www.BabyProfessorBooks.com
to download Free Baby Professor eBooks
and view our catalog of new and exciting
Children's Books